Concert and Contest COLLECTION

Compiled and Edited by **H. VOXMAN**

for

French Horn (in F) with Piano Accompaniment

CONTENTS

RUBANK®

HAL•LEONARD® CORPORATION
7777 W. BLUEMOUND RD. P.O. BOX 13819 MILWAUKEE, WI 53213

Prelude

from Act III of Hérodiade

JULES MASSENET
Transcribed by H. Voxman

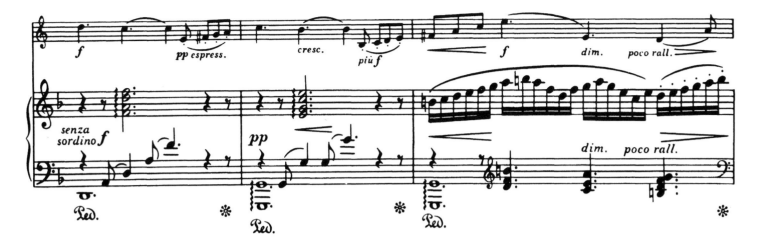

Allerseelen

RICHARD STRAUSS, Op.10, No. 8
Transcribed by H. Voxman

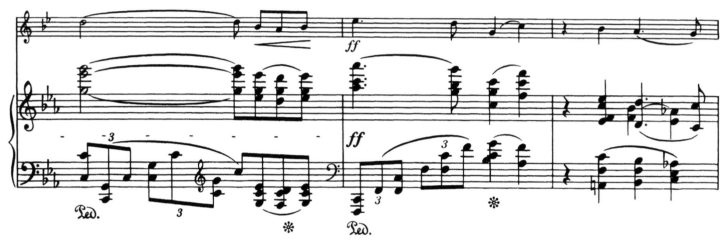

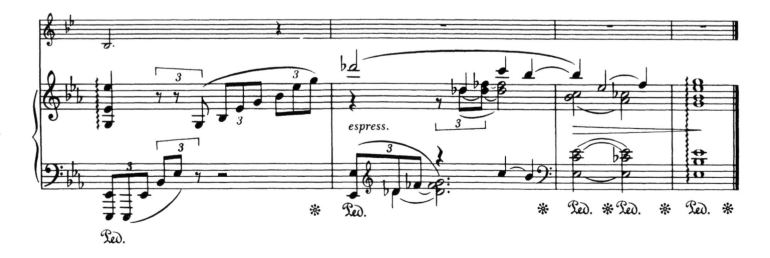

Ballade

LEROY OSTRANSKY

Poco allegretto

Tempo I

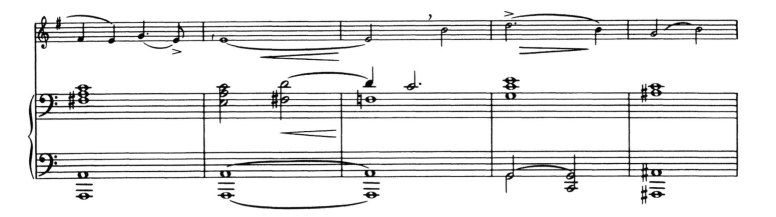

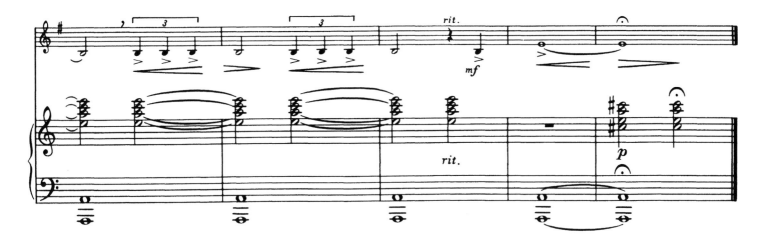

Scherzo

V. SHELUKOV
Transcribed by H. Voxman

Tempo I

Mélodie

CLÉMENT LENOM
Edited by H. Voxman

Farewell Serenade

W. HERFURTH, Op. 85
Edited by H. Voxman

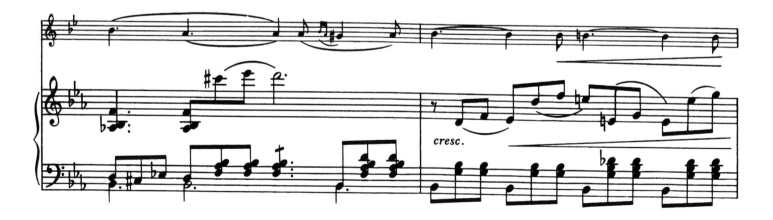

Più Allegro

Nocturne
from A Midsummer Night's Dream

F. MENDELSSOHN
Transcribed by H. Voxman

French Horn (in F)

Piano

* For shorter performance cut from * to *

© Copyright MCMLXI by Rubank, Inc., Chicago, Ill.
International Copyright Secured

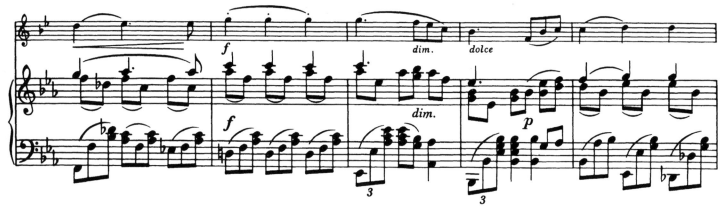

Vocalise

SERGEI RACHMANINOFF
Transcribed by H. Voxman

Lentamente. Molto cantabile

French Horn (in F)

Piano

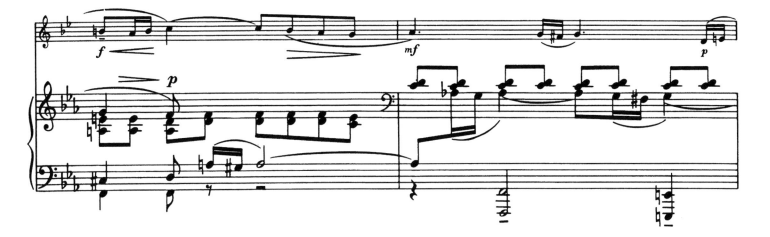

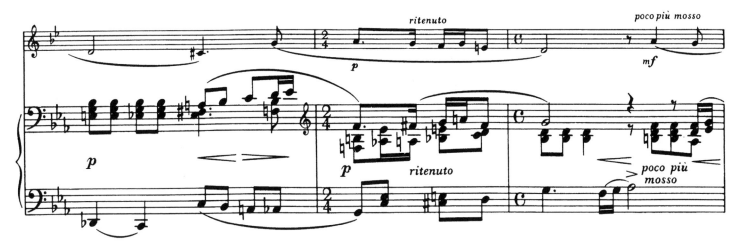

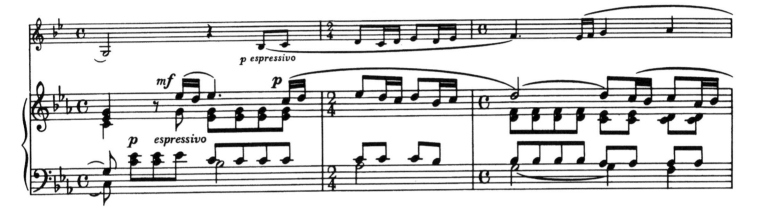

Two Outdoor Scenes

LEROY OSTRANSKY

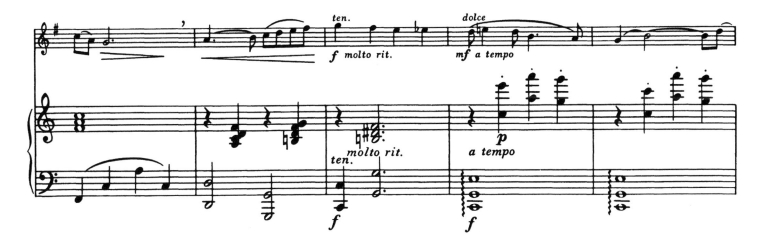

Allegro vivace

Romance

C. SAINT - SAËNS, Op. 36
Edited by H. Voxman

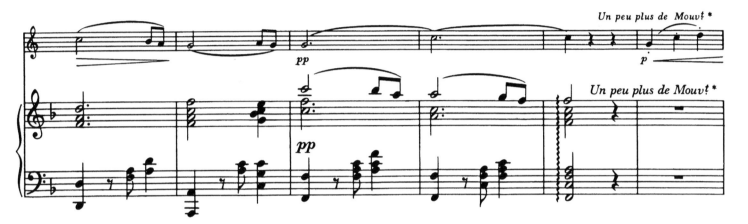

Un peu plus de Mouv! *

* more animated

Rêverie

ALEXANDRE GLAZOUNOW, Op. 24
Edited by H. Voxman

La Chasse

PAUL KOEPKE

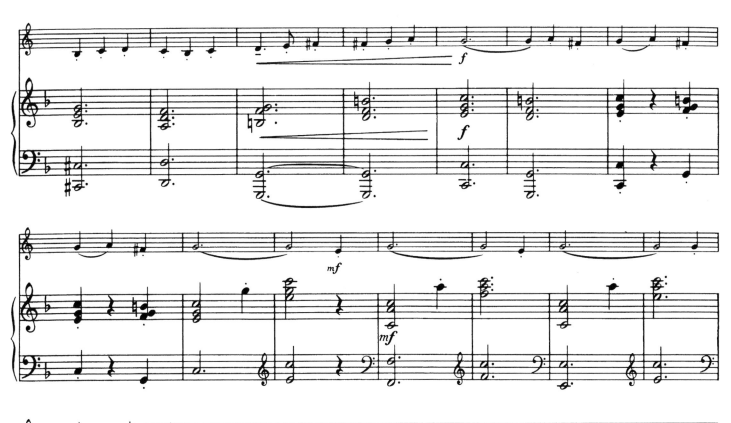

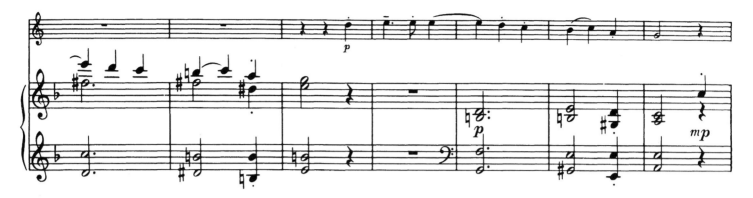

In time, sustained

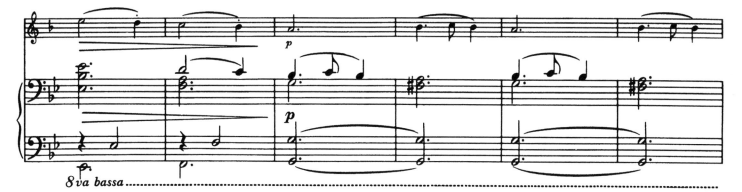

Romanza and Rondo

from Concerto No 4, K. 495

W. A. MOZART
Edited by H. Voxman

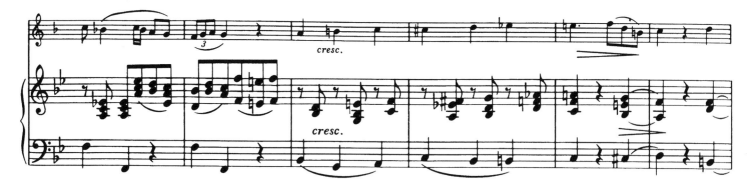

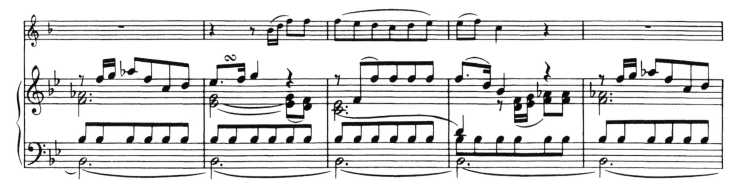

RONDO
Allegro vivace

French Horn (in F)

Piano

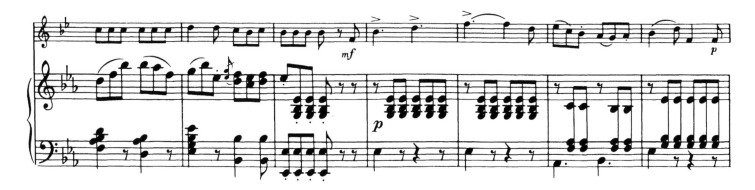

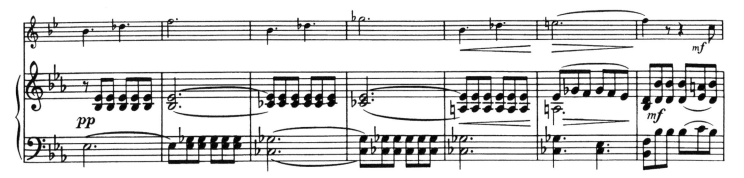

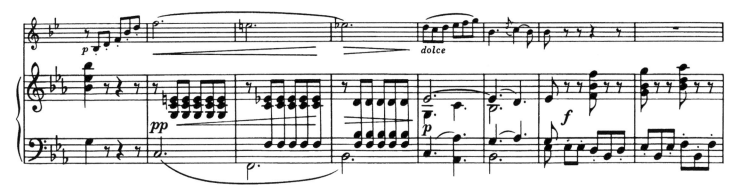

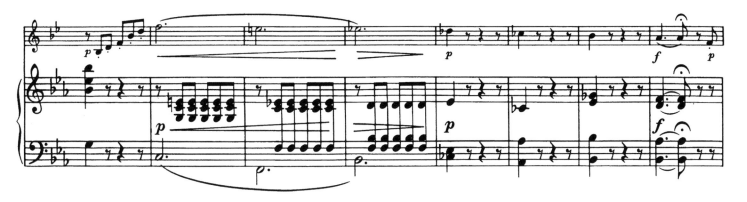

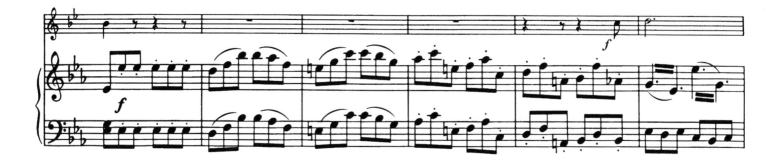

Le Cor

(The Horn)

ANGE FLÉGIER
Transcribed by H. Voxman

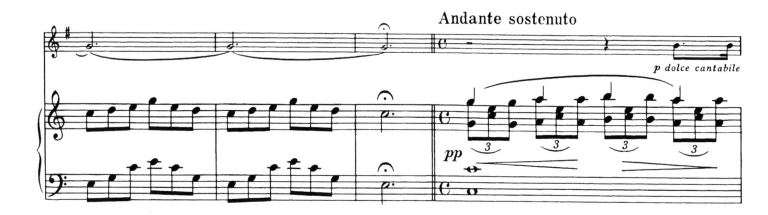

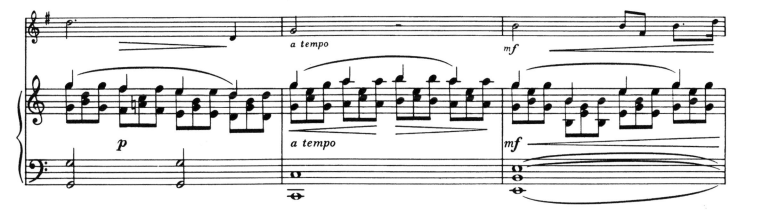

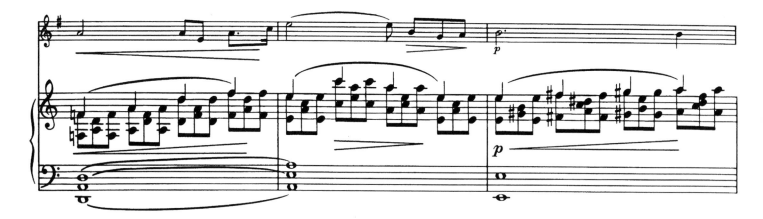

Tempo di marcia funebre

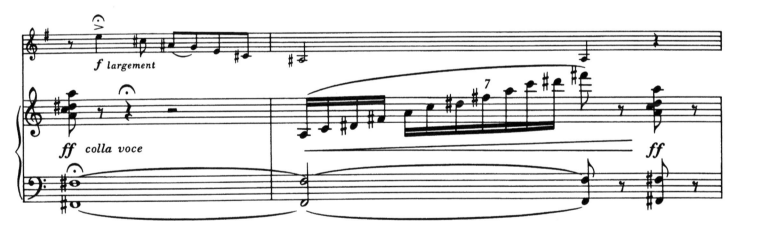

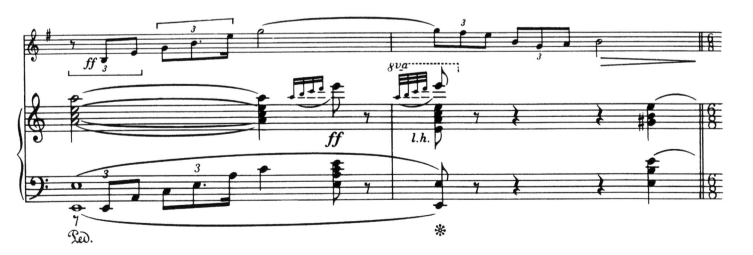